**Dedicated to my wonderful wife
Tina.**

Ubring is a wonderful bull.
He doesn't charge into you with his horns.
He charges your human spirit by looking through his great bullseye,
And seeing into your limitless potential.
And when his massive heart beats in time with yours,
The Perfect Spiral appears in between his horns so you
can see your gifts right in front of you.

You are what Ubring and what Ubring is your gift to the world.

Ubring the bull is the bull in the ring.
And in the ring, you will learn miraculous things.

The miracle of you,
the miracle of me.

The miracle of love that is in everybody.

 A bull named Ubring is calling your name,
Inviting you in to play in the game.

 **The game is The Perfect Spiral and all of us can play.**
The best part is we play together, but in our own way.

As you step in the ring, look into Ubring's eyes.

You will see the infinite universe,
As big as the skies.

If you look very closely, you are one of the stars;
Flickering and fantastic, brighter than Mars.

 And now you are shining in the center of the ring,
And you are the focus of the bull named Ubring.

 As you look to the heavens, Ubring sees into you.
With his great bullseye, he can see what is true.

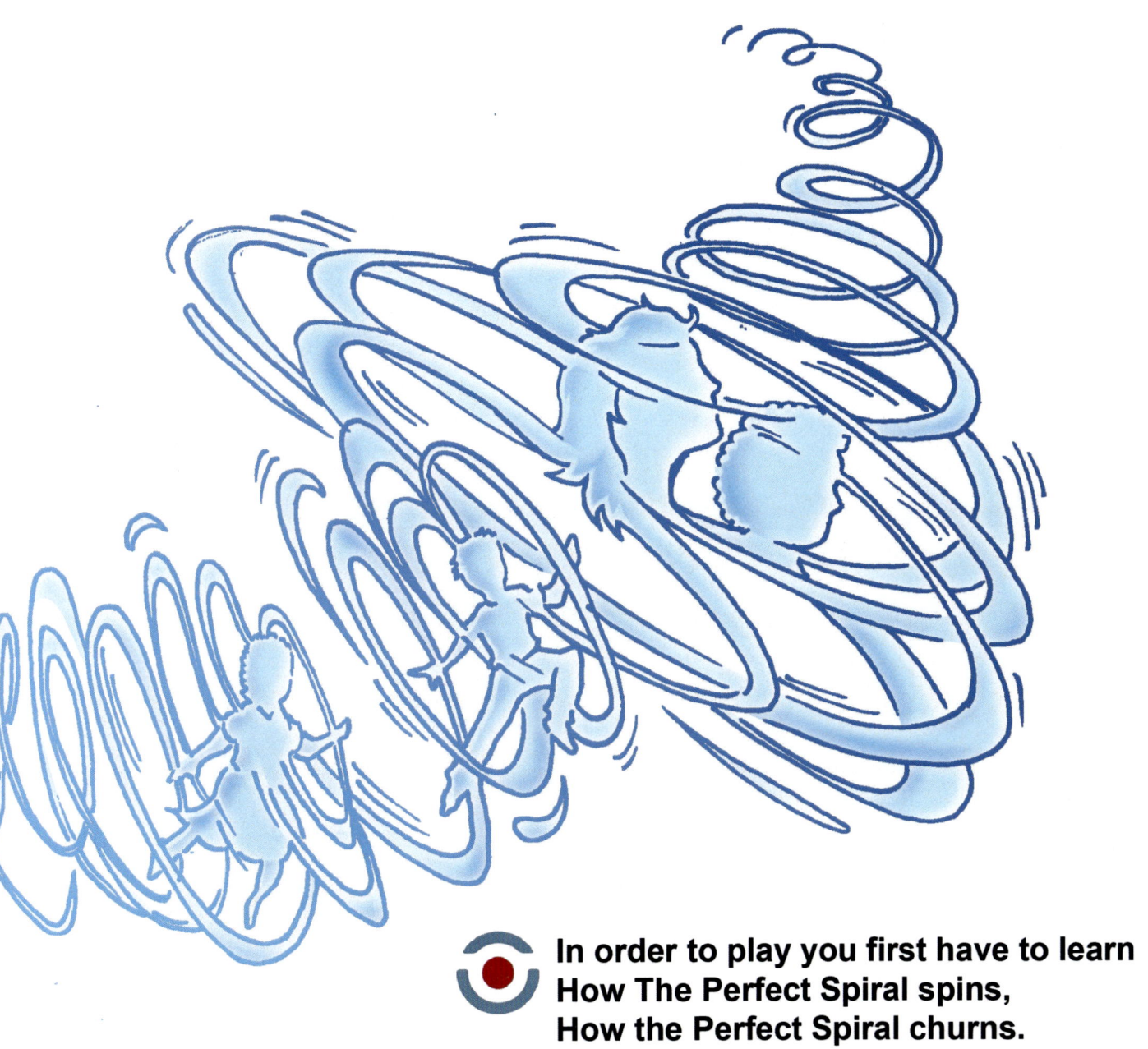

In order to play you first have to learn
How The Perfect Spiral spins,
How the Perfect Spiral churns.

 **There are 7 steps to learning the Perfect Spiral way,
And Ubring will coach you on all 7 of them today.**

Step 1: Chalk it
Step 2: Talk it
Step 3: Walk it
Step 4: Jog it
Step 5: Run it
Step 6: Let it fly
Step 7: Let it play

The first step of learning kicks up all the dust,
That makes up the stars and makes up all of us.

Ubring pounds the dust to the ground
Squeezing it, oh so tight.
The dust turns to chalk, so you and Ubring
Can draw across the night.

The chalk is made of stardust that twinkles in the sky.

Ubring drew The Big Dipper for you,
So your brain will not run dry.

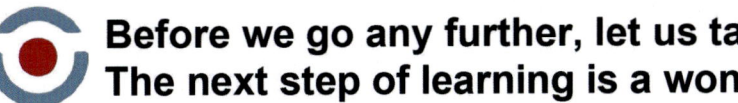

Before we go any further, let us take a sip.
The next step of learning is a wonderful little trip.

 The second step we take, Ubring begins to talk.
As you begin to listen, your brain creates new thoughts.

Ubring will ask you questions
That you can hear in your mind.
These are tiny conversations over
A tiny amount of time.

After the tiny talk, if you listen to every word
Your own ideas will bubble up and fly around like birds.

Before we fly, we have to walk.
This is third way we learn.
Because walking through it
Shows you how to do it,
So the Perfect Spiral turns.

 **As you talk and walk with Ubring**
You will see the spiral spin.

At first, the world begins to wobble
And goose bumps jump on your skin.
And then you will see with your very own eyes
YOU are in the Perfect Spiral,
All of the time.

And when you see it you will shout,
"I am the Perfect Spiral, from the inside out."

The spiral is spinning faster
And picking up the pace.
You can't hold back your laughter
As your heart begins to race.

Ubring begins to jog and you must jog along.
The spiral is spinning faster,
and it's pull is very strong.

What you learn from jogging
Is learning how to think.
You're thinking very quickly now
As Ubring gives a wink.

Ubring starts to run
Faster than you can see.
Charging off into the future
passing us from history.

You think you are standing still,
But your brain is on the run.
Trying to keep up with Ubring,
Isn't learning fun?

Letting your brain run free!
Letting your brain create!

 This is how Ubring charges out of the gate.

Now the thoughts you're thinking
Are flying high with wings.
And you are a miracle making
Because you are what Ubring.

You are the Perfect Spiral,
And these words are all for you.
The only thing you must believe
Is that all of this is true.

Ubring gave you the chalk and you drew across the sky.
Ubring talked and you listened, and you didn't even have to try.

You and Ubring walked and then jogged side by side.
And then you let your brain run free
And oh, what a wonderful ride.

But the ride is just beginning
And the bull named Ubring is grinning.
Because the game isn't about winning
It's about what you have inside.

When the Perfect Spiral flies
It launches all our love.
Ubring's heart is full
With Miracles sent from above.

And all of us are miracles
But it's not enough to say.
We must believe in each other
And then get out of each other's way.

What is the point of The Perfect Spiral,
If you never learned to play?
This is the last lesson to learn
On this miraculous day.

Ubring and you are standing, seeing eye to eye.
If you see the miracle in 'we'
Our eyes will never go blind.

We will see through all the lies.
We will see through all the hate.
And then Our Perfect Spiral will fly
Like it doesn't have any weight.

Ubring isn't your average bull.
Ubring is a matador.
In between his magic horns
You will see the Perfect Spiral soar.

Ubring's horns will charge you
So your human spirit thrives.

When you get out of your way
And let yourself play...

 You will never be more alive.